QUEER AND FEARLESS

POEMS CELEBRATING THE LIVES OF LGBTQ+ HEROES

BY **ROB SANDERS**

ILLUSTRATED BY **HARRY WOODGATE**

Penguin Workshop

TO MY POET FRIENDS WHO INSPIRE,
SUPPORT, AND CHALLENGE ME—LN, HEYS, CBW, AND JY
—RS

TO ALL THOSE WHO INSPIRE
BY LIVING THEIR TRUTH EVERY DAY
—HW

PENGUIN WORKSHOP
An imprint of Penguin Random House LLC, New York

First published in the United States of America by Penguin Workshop,
an imprint of Penguin Random House LLC, New York, 2024

Text copyright © 2024 by Rob Sanders
Illustrations copyright © 2024 by Harry Woodgate

Visit us online at penguinrandomhouse.com.

Library of Congress Cataloging-in-Publication Data is available.

Manufactured in China

ISBN 9780593523698   10 9 8 7 6 5 4 3 2 1 HH

Design by Mary Claire Cruz

CONTENTS

INTRODUCTION

Everyone loves a hero—someone who comes to the rescue or saves the day. This book honors seventeen LGBTQ+ heroes—both activists and politicians. Each of these heroes made a difference for members of the LGBTQ+ community in their own way. LGBTQ stands for Lesbian, Gay, Bisexual, Transgender, Queer and Questioning. The "+" represents anyone else in the community who does not fall under one of those categories.

Real-life heroes are like you and me. They're humans. They're not perfect. Every action they take is not memorable or life-changing. They aren't heroic every day of their lives. But for at least one moment in time, a hero finds the ability to make a difference.

When you think of heroes that way, then it seems possible that we all can become a hero. So, stand up. Speak your mind. Let your truth be known. Make a difference when you can, where you are, and in ways that only you can. Now, be inspired by some of the heroes who came before us.

OUT AND PROUD

Days spun into months and years.
Time for growing hate and fears.
Earth went round and round the sun.
Hard-fought battles. Lost and won.

Listen, hear a quiet song.
Voices whisper: "This is wrong!"
Some thought it could never be—
Equity they longed to see.

Barely heard upon the breeze,
Whistling through the distant trees.
New words rolled in with the tide.
"You are you. Don't run. Don't hide."

Walking through the closet door.
Won't be silent anymore.
Voices calling, brave and loud:
"We are here! We're gay! We're proud!"

PHYLLIS AND DEL PUBLISHED A MAGAZINE

Phyllis Lyon
(she/her)
1924–2020

Del Martin
(she/her)
1921–2008

Phyllis Lyon and
Del Martin—a perfect pair.
Loving. Together.

They helped lesbians
Connect and know each other.
They founded a club.

The club—a safe space.
A place to be who you were.
Friends supporting friends.

Phyllis Lyon and
Del Martin—organizers.
Building. Together.

Social gatherings.
Conversations and debates.
More women joined in.

But how could the club
Reach out to include others?
A newsletter! Yes!

Phyllis Lyon and
Del Martin—now publishers.
Working. Together.

Ideas took shape.
Phyllis and Del led the way.
One step at a time.

Writing. Editing.
Typing, printing, and stapling.
The Ladder was born.

Phyllis Lyon and
Del Martin—two activists.
Leaders. Together.

Essays. Poems. Stories.
News, articles, and advice.
Please accept yourself.

The Ladder gave hope.
Readers learned about themselves.
They were not alone.

Phyllis Lyon and
Del Martin—a perfect pair.
Loving. Together.

Phyllis Lyon and Del Martin met in 1950 and by 1952 had become a couple. They were two of the founders of the Daughters of Bilitis (DOB)—a lesbian social club and the first organization of its kind in the United States. The DOB began in San Francisco, California, in 1955. Phyllis and Del were soon leading the organization and were instrumental in launching *The Ladder*—a magazine—in **October 1956**. At this time, *The Ladder* was the only publication of its kind. Early editions featured book reviews, poems, news, letters from readers, and more.

Over time, the DOB and *The Ladder* took more and more of a political stand. Phyllis and Del did, too. They were the first lesbian couple to be members of the National Organization for Women and continued to be influential feminists and activists in the LGBTQ+ community throughout their lives. They were the first same-sex couple married in the state of California, first in 2004 and then again in 2008.

José Sarria
(he/him)
1922–2013

José Sarria's mother was Colombian, and his father was Spanish. José was the first of his family born in the United States. He studied languages in high school, became an English tutor, served in the army in World War II, and for a while considered becoming a teacher.

At the Black Cat Cafe, a club in San Francisco, José performed songs from famous operas, changing the words to comment on current events. When he performed, he often dressed in gowns and high-heeled shoes with a flower pinned to his dress. José frequently went before the San Francisco Board of Supervisors to complain about police harassment of gays and lesbians. In **1961**, he decided to run for a seat on the Board of Supervisors. José completed the paperwork, filed his application, and began campaigning. A single word was highlighted on his campaign poster—*EQUALITY!*

José was the first openly gay candidate for political office in the United States. On election day, José ended up in ninth place. It was not a victory, but it was a positive step forward for the LGBTQ+ community.

JOSÉ RAN FOR OFFICE

There once was a man who wrote rhymes.
His wordplay was funny at times.
In dresses and heels,
He made great appeals.
But some thought his actions were crimes.

Police anger grew much more heated.
The people were often mistreated.
But what could they do?
Seemed nobody knew.
But our man would not be defeated.

"I've got it!" he said to the crowd,
With flourish he waved and then bowed.
"I'll throw in my name."
Thus, José became
The first who ran gay, out, and proud.

Campaigning with words, charm, and wit,
Some others hoped he would just quit.
José would not bend,
But lost in the end.
A pioneer, all must admit.

There once was a man named José
Who lived his life openly gay.
He was so admired
And others inspired . . .
Campaigning, themselves, to this day.

9

Bayard Rustin
(he/him)
1912–1987

Bayard Rustin was born into a family with African American Methodist and Quaker roots. As a young man he learned what it meant to be discriminated against, both for being Black and for being gay. Bayard studied music, toured with a quartet, and even recorded an album. He became a pacifist (someone who believes war and violence are unacceptable) and a labor organizer. And he was active in civil rights protests.

Bayard traveled to India to study nonviolent protests with those who worked with Mahatma Gandhi. He later shared what he learned with Dr. Martin Luther King Jr. Nonviolence became central to the civil rights movement and other protest movements as well.

Bayard was often discriminated against in the civil rights movement for being gay, but that did not stop him from being one of the key organizers of the March on Washington for Jobs and Freedom on **August 28, 1963**. Throughout his life, Bayard continued to advocate for civil rights, workers' rights, human rights, and gay rights.

BAYARD PLANNED A MARCH

First a boy who liked to sing.
Then a man who moved a King.

Traveled to a far-off land.
Studied protests there, firsthand.

Knowledge gained, the man returned.
Shared with King what he had learned.

Side-by-side for Civil Rights.
Peaceful without any fights.

Planned a march on Washington
In the blazing August sun.

People poured into the mall,
Seeking rights for one and all.

At the march, strong voices grew.
In the crowd, who really knew?

That the man who planned the day
Proudly was both Black and gay.

ERNESTINE WALKED IN A PICKET LINE

Any movement needs a certain number of courageous martyrs.

We want acceptance and we want our rights.

You then decide what you can do.

To me . . . the way to be.

Calling attention to the unjustness.

Come out . . . be strong.

A personal thing.

Become visible.

Ernestine.

Ernestine Eckstein
(she/her)
1941–1992

Born Ernestine Delois Eppenger, in Indiana, she earned a degree in journalism, and then moved to New York City. There, Ernestine realized she was a lesbian and discovered the New York chapter of the Daughters of Bilitis. She soon became the vice president of the organization. In her work as an activist, she began to use the name Ernestine Eckstein.

On **October 23, 1965**, Ernestine joined a picket line outside the White House. It was one of the first protests by members of the LGBTQ+ community. Ernestine was the only Black person in the protest and one of only two women. The sign she carried read "Denial of Equality of Opportunity is Immoral." Ernestine's face is shown in photos from other protests, and she was featured on the cover of *The Ladder* in June 1966. An interview with Ernestine appeared inside the magazine—something almost unheard of at the time. Later, Ernestine moved to California and participated in Black Women Organized for Action and other civil rights organizations.

WE HOMOSEXUALS PLEAD WITH
OUR PEOPLE TO PLEASE HELP
MAINTAIN PEACEFUL AND QUIET
CONDUCT ON THE STREETS OF
THE VILLAGE — MATTACHINE

STORMÉ PROTECTED HER COMMUNITY

Stormé.

Her name was Stormé.

Just like a storm, she was a force
of nature.

Stormé.

Her name was Stormé.

She sang in a baritone voice and
toured Europe.

Stormé.

Her name was Stormé.

She lived in Chicago, then moved to
the eye of the storm—New York City.

Stormé.

Her name was Stormé.

She was the Master of Ceremonies at
the Jewel Box Revue.

Stormé.

Her name was Stormé.

She dressed in men's clothes and
performed as a drag king.

Stormé.

Her name was Stormé.

She was at the Stonewall Inn when a
riot broke out.

Stormé.

Her name was Stormé.

Some say she helped start it all.

Stormé.

Her name was Stormé.

She didn't put up with discrimination
or "ugliness."

Stormé.

Her name was Stormé.

She patrolled the streets of
New York City.

Stormé.

Her name was Stormé.

She continued to protect others into
her seventies.

Stormé.

Her name was Stormé.

Just like a storm, she was a force
of nature.

Stormé DeLarverie
*(she/her;
while performing in drag: he/him)
1920–2014*

Stormé DeLarverie (STORM-ee
de-LAR-ver-ee) was born in New
Orleans to a Black mother and
a white father. She often faced
discrimination for being Black
and for being a lesbian. Early in
her life, she developed a love for
jazz, and by the time Stormé was
fifteen, she was singing in clubs
in her hometown. Soon she was
performing on tour in Europe—
sometimes dressed as a woman,
sometimes as a drag king.

For many years, Stormé was the
host of a traveling show, the Jewel
Box Revue, where she dressed as a
man and performed as a drag king.
She was at the Stonewall Inn when
a riot broke out on **June 28, 1969**.
Some who were there said Stormé
inspired and maybe even started
the riot. Stormé seldom talked
about the event. Later she began to
keep watch on the streets of New
York City to protect queer people
from hate and discrimination,
which Stormé called "ugliness." She
continued to patrol the streets into
her late seventies.

Marsha P. Johnson
(she/her)
1944–1992

Marsha P. Johnson was born in Elizabeth, New Jersey. She knew early in life that she was a transgender woman. Queer and Black, Marsha P. was a minority within a minority. She referred to herself sometimes as a drag queen but later used the term *transgender*.

Marsha P. said the *P* in her name stood for "pay it no mind." She was well known in Greenwich Village, in other neighborhoods around New York City, and in gay clubs. Marsha P. was at the Stonewall Inn on **June 28, 1969**, when the Stonewall Uprising began. The Stonewall Uprising was a riot that lasted several days and was the event many consider the beginning of the modern LGBTQ+ rights movement. Some believe Marsha P.'s actions started the Uprising.

Along with the gay liberation activist Sylvia Rivera, Marsha advocated for transgender rights and created an organization to help homeless trans youth—the first organization of its kind in the United States.

MARSHA P. STARTED AN UPRISING

A drag queen, transgender

Both, she declared

Combing the streets

Dressed in thrift-store finds

Everyone saw Marsha P.

Flowers cascading

Gowns, dresses flowing

Her wig pulled into place

Injustice she witnessed

Jail she endured

Kindness she spread as she went

Living on streets

Minding her business

Not looking for trouble

Others pointed and stared

"**P**ay it no mind"

Quite simply was her reply

Riots broke out

Stonewall, the site

Transgender folks right in the middle

Unafraid, she stood up

Voiced her opinion freely for

Weeks, months, and years . . . then . . .

e**X**tinguished, gone

Yet still remembered—Marsha P.'s

Zest-filled life

Michael McConnell (he/him) 1942– **Jack Baker** (he/him) 1942–

MICHAEL AND JACK SAID "I DO"

I'm Jack.
I'm Michael.

Let's love.
Let's marry.

We will.
But how?

We tried.
Were denied.

Tried again.
Found success.

Set a date.
Planned a wedding.

"I do."
"I do."

"I will."
"I will."

The first.
Forever.

I'm Jack.
I'm Michael.

A couple.
In love.

They met at a Halloween party in Norman, Oklahoma. Their friendship grew into a relationship. When Jack Baker asked Michael McConnell to be his partner, Michael replied, "Only if we can get married." In the 1960s, same-sex marriage was not legal.

When Jack entered law school, he found a loophole in the Minnesota marriage laws. Since the law did not say who could be married, the two men applied for a marriage license. They were told no. They fought the decision in court and their case eventually ended up at the United States Supreme Court, where it was dismissed. Jack had an idea. He changed his name to Pat McConnell. Then Michael went alone to apply for a second marriage license. It was granted.

Jack and Michael were married on **September 3, 1971**. They were the first gay couple legally married in the United States. However, for years, courts in Minnesota refused to record their marriage license. Finally, on September 19, 2018, Michael and Jack's marriage was declared legal "in all respects."

Harvey Milk
(he/him)
1930–1978

Harvey Milk served in the US Navy, worked in finance, served as a public-school teacher, and, for a while, worked on Broadway. When he moved to the Castro District of San Francisco, California, in 1972, Harvey opened a camera shop and soon was organizing the merchants in the district.

Harvey led the formation of the Castro Village Association and planned the first Castro Street Fair to help attract people to local businesses. He worked with others in the LGBTQ+ community and with unions (groups of organized workers) and union leaders to get out the vote. He ran unsuccessfully for office three times. On **November 8, 1977**, on his fourth attempt, he was elected to the San Francisco Board of Supervisors. Harvey was killed, along with Mayor George Moscone, on November 27, 1978. His influence on the LGBTQ+ community continues to this day.

HARVEY ORGANIZED VOTERS

You—Harvey Milk
The New York boy
Who played school sports
Who learned and grew
Who discovered yourself

You—Harvey Milk
The bright young man
Who studied math
Who taught and coached
Who hid yourself

You—Harvey Milk
The working man
Who joined the navy
Who worked on Wall Street
Who searched for yourself

You—Harvey Milk
The San Francisco man
Who owned a shop
Who organized others
Who lived as yourself

You—Harvey Milk
The political man
Who ran and lost
Who found your place
Who was proud of yourself

You—Harvey Milk
The elected man
Who fought for rights
Who tried your best
Who was killed for being yourself

You—Harvey Milk
The remembered man
Who was a hero
Who was gone too soon
Who still helps us be ourselves

Gilbert Baker

(he/him)
1951–2017

Gilbert Baker's grandmother owned a women's clothing store, and more than anything, Gilbert wanted to learn to sew. His dream would not come true until many years later. As an adult, Gilbert joined the army, and eventually was stationed in San Francisco, California, where he found a community of other gay men.

Once he was out of the military and settled into his new life, Gilbert bought a sewing machine. Harvey Milk asked Gilbert to design and create a symbol for the LGBTQ+ community. Gilbert had the idea of a Rainbow Flag that would represent the community and all its members. With the help of volunteers, he cut, dyed, and sewed fabric. The first Rainbow or Pride Flag flew on **June 25, 1978**. Gilbert went on to design other flags and banners. He also worked as an entertainer and was a gay rights activist.

GILBERT DESIGNED A FLAG

The hum-hum-hum of Gilbert's
Grandmother's sewing machine
Fabric and thread merging together
With the rhythmic movements of a needle
Clothes skillfully crafted by hand

As a boy he longed to sew
Boys didn't do such things folks said
Most who knew him thought
he wasn't enough of a boy anyway

The hate-hate-hate of Gilbert's
Classmates and neighbors
Looks and actions merging together
With stinging teasing and torment
Doubt painfully crafted by words

As a young man he longed to sew
But teenagers got drafted
Maybe the army could make him
into the man some thought he wasn't

The hut-hut-hut of army life
Didn't change Gilbert at all
Instead, his work, merging with a city
Helped him discover others like himself
Friendships carefully crafted one by one

As a grown-up he learned to sew
He designed, he created
Sewing let him be who he always was
A man as good as any other

The hum-hum-hum of Gilbert's
Very own sewing machine
Fabric and thread merging together
With the rhythmic movements of a needle
A symbol lovingly crafted with friends

As a community they came together
They marched, they cheered
A waving rainbow led the way
Gilbert's flag was for them all

CLEVE CREATED A QUILT

Cleve

Nonviolent   Gay

Interning   Demonstrating   Leading

Activist   Organizer   Creator   Founder

Speaking   Inspiring   Challenging

Equality-champion

Jones

Quilt

Warmth   Comfort

Cutting   Piecing   Sewing

Memories   Families   Celebration   Protest

Unfolding   Displaying   Remembering

Emotional   Powerful

Monument

Cleve Jones
(he/him)
1954–

Cleve Jones was no stranger to bullying and harassment during high school. At eighteen, he told his parents he was gay. They weren't happy. Like many young gay men in the 1970s, he moved to San Francisco, California. Cleve quickly made friends in the city.

In the early eighties, the crisis of AIDS—a disease that had a huge and deadly impact on the gay community—began. Cleve soon cofounded the San Francisco AIDS Foundation. He had the idea for what would become the NAMES Project AIDS Memorial Quilt in 1985 during a candlelight memorial. Looking at the names of those who had died of AIDS written on pieces of cardboard taped to a building, Cleve remembered the quilt his grandmother once created. He made the first panel for the AIDS Memorial Quilt in **1987** in honor of his friend Marvin Feldman, who had died of AIDS.

The AIDS Memorial Quilt became both a memorial and a protest. The Quilt is one of the largest public art projects in the world, which has been seen by millions. Cleve Jones continues his activism to this day.

PAULINE WORKED FOR EQUALITY

Who gets adopted?

What does it feel like to leave one country for another?

Where is the United States?

When does someone know who they are?

Why does a five-year-old understand, when no one else does?

How do you tell people you are a girl?

Who grows up hoping to live their truth?

What does it feel like when people don't understand?

Where do you go to find acceptance?

When is it time to choose a new name?

Why does someone become an activist?

How does one begin?

Who? Pauline Park.

What? A Korean American trans activist.

Where? New York City.

When? From the time she was five.

Why? To ensure rights for herself and others.

How? One step at a time.

Pauline Park
(she/her)
1960–

Adopted from Korea by European American parents, Pauline Park knew by an early age that she was a transgender woman. At the age of thirty-six, she transitioned to be her true self. The process was not easy, and not everyone accepted her. After seeing and experiencing discrimination in New York City, Pauline became an activist. She is best known for fighting for rights associated with identity and expression.

Most of Pauline's work focused on protecting trans people from discrimination at work, school, and in doctor's offices and hospitals. In **2002**, Pauline led the campaign to include transgender rights in New York City's human rights law. She also successfully led the campaigns for the Dignity for All Schools Act, which was enacted in New York City in 2004 and in the state of New York in 2012. In 2004, Pauline was the first openly transgender person to serve as grand marshal in the New York City Pride March.

RICHARD READ A POEM

He was
One immigrant
One Latino
One gay man
One poet

Richard wrote a poem
A poem for a **president**
A poem for a **nation**
A poem for his **mother**
A poem for his **husband**
A poem for all of **us**

Richard read a poem
Read to the **president**
Read to a **nation**
Read to his **mother**
Read to his **husband**
Read to all of **us**

One sun   **One** ground
One sky   **One** country
One people   **One** poem
One immigrant   **One** Latino
One gay man   **One** poet

Richard Blanco
(he/him)
1968–

Richard Blanco was born in Madrid, Spain, where his Cuban parents had immigrated. The family soon immigrated to the United States, and Richard grew up in Miami, Florida. He became a civil engineer but always loved writing and soon pursued his dreams of being a poet.

Richard quickly accepted when asked to be the poet for President Barack Obama's second inauguration. He was the fifth poet in history to receive the honor of being an inaugural poet. Richard would be the youngest, first openly gay, first immigrant, and first Cuban American poet to compose and read a poem at a presidential inauguration. What it means to be an American was often a theme in Richard's poetry, and his inaugural poem would explore that theme, too. He had two to three weeks to write and submit three poems for consideration. The inaugural committee selected his poem "One Today."

On **January 21, 2013**, Richard looked out on the crowd of hundreds of thousands of people, as millions more watched on television. He read his poem about what it means to be an American, representing Americans who seldom, if ever, had been represented—immigrants, gays, and Cuban Americans.

Jeff Tiller
(he/him)
1983–

Aditi Hardikar
(she/her)
1989–

Jeff Tiller and Aditi Hardikar made history the day they started working for President Barack Obama in the White House. Jeff was Director of Specialty Media, including LGBTQ+ outreach, and Aditi worked as associate director of the White House Office of Public Engagement and White House liaison to the LGBTQ+ community. They were part of the largest LGBTQ+ presence in any president's administration.

Knowing the Supreme Court of the United States' (SCOTUS) decision on marriage equality was soon coming, Jeff had the idea to light the North Portico of the White House (also known as the president's front door) in the colors of the Pride Flag. Aditi quickly joined the project, and together, the two gained the support of others in the White House. On **June 26, 2015**, when the SCOTUS announced their decision in favor of marriage equality, President Obama gave the go-ahead to turn on the lights. Jeff, Aditi, and others—including Michelle Obama and daughter Malia—watched as the White House glowed in the colors of the rainbow.

JEFF AND ADITI LIT A RAINBOW

Marriage equality—hot debate.
Loving couples had to wait.
Could the White House glow with pride?
What would happen if no one tried?

Questions, ideas in a meeting.
One idea quickly fleeting.
Would a decision at last be made?
Or would hope begin to fade?

One man walked out from that meeting—
Talking, texting, and then tweeting.
Who will make it real—this dream?
Allies, partners joined Jeff's team.

Aditi stepped up. And others did, too.
Plans were made. The excitement grew.
Would the judgment soon be made?
Could the president's mind be swayed?

June 26, the ruling announced.
Marriage equality was pronounced.
Could the White House show the display?
Would the president give his okay?

Daytime slowly turned to night.
North Portico transformed with light.
Rainbow shown upon the wall.
Marriage equality, now for all.

Pete Buttigieg

(he/him)

1982–

A native of South Bend, Indiana, Pete Buttigieg grew up, went to college, traveled the world, and decided to run for public office. His hard work and determination led to his election as mayor of his hometown. Pete served in Afghanistan as an officer in the United States Navy Reserves. He came out and told the world he was gay while running for reelection. Pete won his second term by a landslide and soon married Chasten Glezman.

On **April 14, 2019**, Pete announced his candidacy for president of the United States, becoming the first out and proud gay candidate for the Democratic nomination and the first candidate married to a partner of the same sex. He even won the Iowa caucuses and placed a close second in the New Hampshire primary. Pete eventually dropped out of the race. He went on to serve in President Joe Biden's cabinet, becoming the first openly gay cabinet secretary in US history. Pete and Chasten are the fathers of two children.

PETE RAN FOR PRESIDENT

Buttons—Banners—Bumper stickers.

T-shirts—Town Hall Meetings—TV appearances.

The signs were everywhere. The signs were for Pete.

Signs of an election. Signs of the times.

Mayor Pete

Pete Buttigieg for America

Vote Pete—President 2020

Can't Beat Pete

Freedom

Democracy

Security

A fresh start for America

Team Pete 2020

BOOT-EDGE-EDGE

BOOT-EDGE-EDGE

BOOT-EDGE-EDGE

Mayor Pete for President

A President for Our Generation

Freedom—Democracy—Security

Pete & Chasten

This is what love looks like!

Pride for Pete

#Family

GLOSSARY

bisexual · a person who is attracted to both men and women, or to people of various gender identities

closet door · figuratively used to represent the barriers that keep LGBTQ+ individuals from being open about their identities

drag king · an entertainer (typically a woman or nonbinary person) who performs while impersonating a man through clothing and makeup

drag queen · an entertainer (typically a man or nonbinary person) who performs while impersonating a woman through clothing and makeup

gay · a person who is attracted to a person of the same sex

hero · a person known for courageous acts

LGBTQ+ · lesbian, gay, bisexual, transgender, queer/questioning, intersex, asexual/aromantic/agender—the + is a way of including others who are in the community but may not be or feel represented within the categories of LGBTQ

lesbian · a female or nonbinary person who is attracted to other women

martyr · a person who gives up their life for what they believe

out · self-identifying one's sexual orientation or gender identity personally or publicly

queer · any person whose sexuality or gender identity falls outside the heterosexual mainstream or the gender binary

questioning · the Q in LGBTQ+ can also refer to those who are questioning, exploring, learning, or experimenting with their sexual or romantic orientation or gender identity

transgender · a person whose gender identity differs from the sex they were assigned at birth

A WORD ABOUT PRONOUNS

Today, individuals often specify which pronouns they use and that others should use when referring to them. Historically, it's not always possible to establish what a person's pronouns were or might have been. In this book we have used interviews with individuals, their writing, and other sources to establish pronouns as accurately as possible.

ABOUT THE POEMS

"Out and Proud," page 5
Quatrain—A quatrain is any poem of four lines. This quatrain has four stanzas, each with two sets of rhyming couplets.

"Phyllis and Del Published a Magazine," page 7
Senryu—Like a haiku, a senryu features three lines of five, seven, and five syllables. Instead of focusing on nature as in a haiku, a senryu focuses on human nature. This poem is a series of thirteen senryu poems.

"José Ran for Office," page 9
Limerick—A limerick is a five-line poem that is known for its bouncy rhythm. A limerick follows the rhyme scheme AABBA. This poem is a series of five limericks.

"Bayard Planned a March," page 10
Rhyming Couplet—A couplet is a two-line poem or stanza that rhymes. This poem has eight rhyming couplets. It could also be called a double quatrain.

"Ernestine Walked in a Picket Line," page 11
Cento—A cento poem uses lines from another poet and arranges them in a different way. This poem uses actual quotes from Ernestine.

"Stormé Protected Her Community," page 13
Free Verse with Repeated Phrases—A free verse poem does not use rhyme or meter. This poem shows how phrases can be repeated when creating a free verse poem.

"Marsha P. Started an Uprising," page 14
Abecedarian—An abecedarian is a poem arranged alphabetically.

"Michael and Jack Said 'I Do,'" page 15
Duet—A duet poem is designed for two people to read alternating lines, thus creating a duet or pair of voices.

"Harvey Organized Voters," page 16
Poem of Address—In a poem of address, the poet writes as if speaking to a person or object.

"Gilbert Designed a Flag," page 19
Free Verse—A free verse poem does not use rhyme or meter. It often sounds like natural speech, but uses sounds, images, and literary devices in an artistic way.

"Cleve Created a Quilt," page 21
Diamante—A diamante poem is a seven-line poem that forms the shape of a diamond. The first and last lines use one word each, which are usually opposites. The second and sixth lines use two adjectives, the third and fifth lines use three verbs, and the fourth line uses four nouns. The first half of the diamante describes the first line, and the last half of the diamante describes the last line.

"Pauline Worked for Equality," page 22
Question Poem—Question poetry asks one question after another to create a powerful and emotional tone.

"Richard Read a Poem," page 25
Shape Poem—A shape poem is a poem that is shaped like the thing it describes. The shape can also add additional meaning to the poem.

"Jeff and Aditi Lit a Rainbow," page 27
Hybrid Poem—A hybrid poem mixes styles and forms of poetry. This poem mixes a quatrain with a question poem.

"Pete Ran for President," page 28
Found Poem—A found poem is made by taking words and phrases from other sources, such as newspapers, signs, or menus, and arranging them into a poem. This poem uses signs, banners, bumper stickers, and other items seen when Pete was campaigning for president.

AUTHOR'S NOTE

I grew up learning about history. The history of my family, the history of my hometown and state, the history of the United States, and even the history of my religion. But I never learned the history of the LGBTQ+ community to which I was discovering I belonged. Ironically, that history was happening all around me from the time I was in elementary school in the 1960s, through high school graduation in 1977, and then through college, graduate school, and beyond. I seldom heard or read news stories about gays, lesbians, and transgender people who were standing up, speaking out, and demanding equality. For a long time, I never knew there were allies— people who were not gay, lesbian, or transgender—who were working on behalf of my community. I benefited from the actions and sacrifices of these activists, politicians, and allies, however. All of us have, whether we're part of the LGBTQ+ community or not.

This book celebrates the actions of seventeen LGBTQ+ political and social activists. There are hundreds more, perhaps thousands. Some of their names and contributions are known. Others have been lost to history. The most important thing a book like this can do is to help a reader want to know more. I hope you will begin to search for other LGBTQ+ heroes you can celebrate.

ADDITIONAL READING

Gay & Lesbian History for Kids: The Century-Long Struggle for LGBT Rights, with 21 Activities by Jerome Pohlen (Chicago Review Press, 2016)

Mayor Pete: The Story of Pete Buttigieg by Rob Sanders, illustrated by Levi Hastings (Henry Holt and Company, 2020)

No Way, They Were Gay? Hidden Lives and Secret Loves by Lee Wind (Zest Books, 2021)

Pride: The Story of Harvey Milk and the Rainbow Flag by Rob Sanders, illustrated by Steven Salerno (Random House, 2018)

Queer, There, and Everywhere: 23 People Who Changed the World by Sarah Prager, illustrated by Zoë More O'Ferrall (HarperCollins, 2017)

Song for the Unsung: Bayard Rustin, the Man Behind the 1963 March on Washington by Carole Boston Weatherford and Rob Sanders, illustrated by Byron McCray (Henry Holt and Company, 2022)

Stitch by Stitch: Cleve Jones and the AIDS Memorial Quilt by Rob Sanders, illustrated by Jamey Christoph (Magination Press, 2021)

Stonewall: A Building. An Uprising. A Revolution. by Rob Sanders, illustrated by Jamey Christoph (Random House, 2019)

This Day in June by Gayle E. Pitman, illustrated by Kristyna Litten (Magination Press, 2014)

Two Grooms on a Cake: The Story of America's First Gay Wedding by Rob Sanders, illustrated by Robbie Cathro (Little Bee Books, 2021)

When You Look Out the Window: How Phyllis Lyon and Del Martin Built a Community by Gayle E. Pitman and Christopher Lyles (Magination Press, 2017)